Flowers

These Are Your Flowers

By Mark L Baynard

Life Has Meaning Series

Book One

These Are Your Flowers
Copyright © 2015 – Mark L Baynard

2015 © In Pursuit of Freedom Publishing

All rights reserved. No part of this work covered by the copyright herein may be reproduced, transmitted, stored, or used in any form or by any means, electronic or mechanic including photocopying, recording, or otherwise, without written permission from the author or the publisher.

Printed in the United States

The names of the characters in this book have been changed in order to protect the innocent!

ISBN 13: 978-0-9861380-2-7

ISBN 10: 0986138029

Library of Congress Control Number 2015912125

Editor: Mark L Baynard, In Pursuit of Freedom Publishing
Back Cover Photo: Tommy Watkins, photosnowunlimited@yahoo.com
Book Cover Design: Ida Jannson for Amygdala Designs, amagdaladesign.net

Contact Information:
mark100years@yahoo.com

Website: www.journey100years.com

Books by the Author: Mark L Baynard
These Are Your Flowers
    (Life Has Meaning Series: Book One)
100 Years: A Journey to End a Vicious Cycle

Social Networks:
Twitter: www.twitter.com/mark100years
Facebook Page www.facebook.com/mark100years
FB Page: www.facebook.com/journey100years
YouTube http://www.youtube.com/c/MarkBaynard
Author Page: www.amazon.com/-/e/B00TLXK5L6
LinkedIn: www.linkedin.com/in/MarkBaynard
Goodreads www.goodreads.com/mark100years
Instagram www.instagram.com/mark100years
Pinterest: www.pinterest.com/mark100years
Periscope www.periscope.tv/mark100years
Google+ @mark100years

In Pursuit of Freedom Publishing

"Sometimes we neglect to take the time to let our loved ones know just how much they mean to us. There is a need to give those individuals their flowers while they are still alive."

Mark L Baynard

"These Are Your Flowers"

Dedication

I would like to dedicate this book to everyone who has a special loved one in their life. Both of my grandmothers initially come to my mind. They have each given me their all in an effort to assist in making my life better. My grandmother on my mother's side of the family is no longer with us. She passed on many years ago while I was sitting in prison serving time on a drug conviction. Due to being in prison, I was not allowed to attend her funeral. My grandmother on my dad's side of the family has and continues to live a long life. I now use the knowledge and wisdom which they both attempted to give me many years ago. When they may have thought that I wasn't listening, their words were hidden in my heart until the day that my mind became mature enough to digest it. I can't forget my mother, step mother, my dad, my wife and others. I now dedicate this book as a small token to you all. I hope this book will add meaning to our relationships. These Are Your Flowers! Life Has Meaning Series: Book One!

Table of Contents

Acknowledgments
Introduction
Chapters
1   Positive Influences
2   These Three Individuals
3   85th Birthday Celebration
4   The Value of Family
5   Thank You!
6   Here's Your Flowers

Outro
Books by the Author
About the Author
Life Has Meaning
References

Acknowledgement

I would like to acknowledge those who assisted in making this possible. Being an author is a gift and I thank the Most High God for giving me the strength and courage to reach for my goals. I take this profession serious and I hope that my words can help others in their daily lives. I thank my wife for her patience and understanding while I worked on this book. I also thank my wife for helping me in this process and for the encouraging words. I am humbled and honored to call you my wife!

These Are Your

Flowers

Introduction

"These Are Your Flowers" is the first book in the "Life Has Meaning Series." This series was established in an attempt to look into ways of improving the way we think about life. My goal is to shed light on relevant issues which we may have the opportunity to address concerning our communities. My hope is that this series will encourage and motivate others to become better human beings. There is a need to bring more light into our world. Change sometimes happens in very small stages. None of us are perfect but we all have an opportunity to walk in a direction which may set a positive example for others. There are gifts within each of us, and I look forward to the fruit which will be produced.

"These Are Your Flowers" is purposed to encourage us all as individuals, to give our loved ones their flowers while they are alive. It's important to say the things that we need to say to them before it's too late. After one has passed on, our opportunity to say or do anything else with them is gone.

The gift of life is our most delicate privilege that we are able to enjoy for an undetermined amount of time. No one actually knows the day or time that our lives may suddenly come to an end. I have heard elders say that this journey will go by quicker than our minds can imagine. Even though I used the word "enjoy" to describe our time here on earth, there may be difficult times along the way. There may appear to be more difficult times than there are enjoyable times for some. Life, as we now know it, will eventually come to an end. Time continues to expire even as I write this book. There will come a time that we will leave our loved ones here on earth to figure things out on their own. This is a hard but true statement.

For the ones passing on, their hope may be that they left some meaningful advice and gave proper guidance. They may also hope that they were able to leave a little financial support for immediate family members. For the ones left behind, losing a loved one can be a very sad day. They are usually dealing with a number of raw emotions. Some of these emotions are derived from guilt or the hurt of losing someone. In some case it's not only losing someone but losing the person whom we love most. Then there's the reality of dealing with not having the opportunity or time to say good bye. My grandmother on my mother's side of the family passed on while I was sitting in a prison on a drug conviction. I can say without shame that this was very hurtful to me.

This was due to the choices which I've made in my life. As a result, I was not able to say goodbye to my grandmother. She did not see all of the progress that I've made in my life after being released from prison. I do believe that she would have been proud of me as I have developed into a responsible man.

During funerals family and friends come together in order to show support and pay respect to the individual.

Funerals can be very emotional as everyone gets their last chance to mourn before the burial. There will be tears, some may even yell or scream. This is a time to release some of the hurt bottled up on the inside. During the funeral the preacher usually focuses on the dash between the date of birth and the date of passing. This very small dash represents the entire journey of life in which the individual lived. The preacher will highlight a few good points in order to offer peace to the remaining family members. There may be a time set aside where individuals may stand up and share testaments of how the person benefited their life. Others will leave flowers, in order to show the love that they have for this individual. This is a good thing for others to come out and show support for anyone who have passed on. This causes me to think about the person receiving this love and support after passing on. Were those sentiments of love expressed to this individual while they were living? This brings me to the thought of giving our loved ones their "flowers" while they are still here on earth. This is the very thing that brings me to the purpose of writing this book. Giving flowers is a great thing but how much more if they can see them, smell them, feel them, and appreciate them.

I hope that my readers will be encouraged to express their love and adoration for their loved ones while they are alive and able to feel and appreciate those flowers. A question which I would like to ask my readers are: would you want your flowers while here on earth or would you prefer to receive those flowers while eternally sleeping in a casket? I'm just saying.

These Are Your Flowers

Life Has Meaning Series:

Book One

These Are Your Flowers

Chapter 1

Positive Influences

There are positive influences which may cross our paths, thereby making life just a little easier for us. In some cases these individuals live their lives without knowing whether or not they were appreciated. When I reflect over my life, I come to this very question? Where would I be, if it were not for the many positive influential individuals in my life? There are times in my life when I have to pause or stop everything that I'm doing and say "thank you!" I don't feel a sense of entitlement because I know the many mistakes that I've made. I also know that I didn't make it this far in life without help. In my case, I had a lot of help along the way. Those positive influences helped me in more ways than anyone can imagine. There were a number of times when I reflected back on words that were said to me as a child, in order to deal with current situations. I have to consider myself to be blessed despite the many failures that I've experienced. There are more people than I have room to name in this book. I decided to add only a few so that this book may come to an end.

I think about how actors or other celebrities stand up at an awards show and pull out a long sheet of paper while accepting an award. Written on the sheet of paper is usually a list of all of the people that they would like to thank for assisting in making their careers better. If I were to name every individual for assisting in molding and shaping me into the man that I have become, I would also have a long list. I would even have to leave room for the ones who helped me through prayers and encouraging words. Besides the many individuals who've helped me intentionally, there are those who helped me unintentionally.

Those who are walking around healthy today may not be here tomorrow. This is just a reality which we must all live with. It can be difficult to lose a loved one. I understand this clearly! When we lose a loved one or should I say when they pass on, we have a tradition in our society to give them flowers during the funeral. Several things take place during this time. Funeral are an attempt to give family members closure while also respectfully bringing a close to a person's life. Families are usually brought closer together while dealing with the lost. They come from far and near for this special day. When I think on these things, I understand that funerals are necessary. I noticed that in most cases, we only honor our loved ones after they pass on. I think it would be a great idea if we were to give the ones who mean so much to us, their flowers while they are alive and well. I think that they would appreciate this act of love and kindness. Why wait until they are dead and gone before giving them flowers and just saying "I Love You" or "Thank You" for all that you've done for us.

I have flowers to give out in this book. There have been a number of people who have contributed to my life. For each of them, I would like to give them their flowers while they are alive and well. I will start by saying "thank you" to everyone. To name a few: My dad, my mother, my step mother, my wife, aunts, uncles, my grandmother, aunts, uncles and many others are all deserving of flowers. I would like to show my appreciation to these individuals.

I can clearly remember Ms. Tee and the many kind acts that she had shown me. She was more like family and contributed to my life when I was around four or five years old. There were plenty of times when Ms. Tee would allow me to ride with her when she went in town to the store. This was beneficial to me because Ms. Tee would sometimes buy me a small treat, of my choice. Living deep within a country area, at the time, I had the opportunity to see stores and other sights while with her. I also enjoyed riding with Ms. Tee and sharing time with her. My family still laugh at the silly words that I used to say when I got angry with Ms. Tee. Reflecting back, I understand that this is not a laughing matter. I now apologize for those times that I said "I hope that she drives off a cliff" when she didn't take me with her. Ms. Tee had a special place for me in her heart when I was a young child. The time and love that

Ms. Tee invested in me had a positive impact on my life. It feels good to be wanted, needed, and appreciated. I really appreciate being cared for and showed loved by a person as sweet as Ms. Tee. Ms. Tee, I thank you and appreciate all that you've done for me and how you contributed to my life. Many years have passed since those days but I continue to appreciate her. Ms. Tee is still with us here on earth and I would like to offer this chapter as a small token of all that she has done for me. I reach these flowers to you in the form of this chapter in this book. These are your flowers!

Chapter 2

These Three Individuals

I am very humbled and appreciative to be given the opportunity to give flowers to my loved ones. These three individuals are people that I hold very close to my heart! They have continued to be there for me throughout my life. Despite the many mistakes which I have made, they have been there for me. I have failed them many times, yet they continued to stand by my side. These three individuals who I speak of are my mother, my step-mother, and my dad. I appreciate, respect and honor you all as individuals. I would like to say thank you to each of these magnificent individuals. I know that you deserve more than I am able to give. I've already expressed my thanks to each of them in person but I wanted to restate those sentiments in this book.

My life has gone through a number of different events. I've made a number of irresponsible decisions which placed my life in dangerous situations many times over. By the grace of God, I am still here to breathe and see another day.

During my childhood these three individuals, along with others, have played a significant role in shaping the man that I've become. I'm especially appreciative of these three wonderful individuals and all that they've done for me. One of my earliest memories consists of my dad and my step mother. We were living in Spain as my dad was serving his country while in the military. We had an apartment which was nicely furnished. My younger brother, my sister, my dad and my step mother were there. My step mother took care of us while my dad was at work. I've learned a lot from her while there. I can remember attending school in Spain and learning to speak Spanish. She helped me with my spelling words and other school work. We often went to a huge open Market, I am guessing to purchase things. I remember that there were a lot of merchants who sold all kinds of merchandise there. There were a lot of Knick Knacks that we had in our apartment which my dad may have purchased at the market. I remember there were two large swords that hung on our wall, in the apartment, across one another. These may have been purchased from the market also.

My dad usually came home tired from a hard day's work. Even while being tired, he made time for the family. We had a number of family events and also did a lot of traveling. I also remember going to a number of different restaurants eating good meals. Other times, my step mother prepared our meals and we ate at the table as a family. My dad was the provider, disciplinarian and leader of the family. Being a quick learner himself, he expected us to learn as he taught us many lessons about life. He led by example and made his expectations clear.

My dad has been a part of my life even during the years when I lived with my mother in Delaware. In addition to sending for me to visit him in Alabama once or twice a year, he would send money on occasions. No, my dad is not a perfect man! He has something in common with the rest of us, which are flaws. We all have flaws which can be a gift to keep us humble. I learned a lot about life from my dad.

I see my dad as having such qualities as courage, determination and the will to accomplish whatever he sets his mind to do. I have adopted some of those qualities in my own life. I can say that I am a better man and a more responsible father as a result. I am open to continue to grow and learn new things about life and myself. I am thankful for my dad. During the movie "Lean on Me," I remember one of the students saying something that stuck with me for a long time. The students had grown to love and appreciate Mr. Clark, the school Principal, for the work he had done. Mr. Clark had done a magnificent job with his students. He motivated them to work harder on their assignments and reach for their goals (Lean on Me, 1989). He also improved the physical appearance of the school. His methods may have been unorthodox, but the results were an increase in grade point average and a higher graduation rate. After being arrested for chaining the doors of the school, students of the school formed a protest for the return of Mr. Clark as Principal. They chanted "we want Mr. Clark." There was a lady who attempted to convince the students that the board would find them a good principal. One of the students spoke these words with confidence, "We don't want a good Principal we want Mr. Clark." I understand the student's words clearly. I can imagine myself standing there saying, "I don't want a good dad, I want my own dad!" Thanks pop for everything that you've done for me and the family!

My biological mother is a very sweet lady as well. She has been and continues to be a very hard worker. During my childhood, I don't remember her making excuses for her financial situation. One thing that she did well was "making ends meet" with the very little that she had. My mother made many sacrifices for her children, so that our lives would be better. I remember when she worked as a nurse's aide while caring for the elderly. Her job responsibilities consisted of cleaning their rooms and taking care of them on a daily basis. She was also required to bathe them.

This included wiping them when they used the bathroom on themselves.

I believe that my mother was motivated by the will to take care of her children while at work. I believed that she must have reminded herself of her responsibility to her children each time she had to clean one of her patience. I have many fond memories and examples of the love that she has shown us. Her priorities were in the right place as she considered her children in everything that she did. I can honestly say that I do see my mother as being a positive example of courage. Her life can be used as an example of not giving up despite how bad things were. She didn't attend church much at the time but she was connected to God. I've seen her cry a number of times as she prayed to God. I must say that I have a better understanding about love because of my mother. I learned so much while being raised by her. She gave so much of herself. There was so much love within our household. We were happy as a family even without financial stability.

My life is where it is today because of the many chances that these three individuals have given me. Despite my many failures, they refused to give up on me but instead saw hope when there was none.

To my dad, my step mother, and my biological mother; this is a very small token but I thank you all for all that you've done for me. I love and appreciate you! I give these flowers to you in the form of this chapter. Thank you for everything! These are you flowers!

Chapter 3

85th Birthday Celebration

This was destined to be a great day with an amazing cause. There are times in our lives when everything else around us must temporarily come to a pause. Some of these events consist of a wedding, graduation ceremony, purchasing a new home and a funeral. This event did not consist of any of the things that I mentioned but it was a day worth mentioning. I can remember the events from start to finish. The energy within the room was full of excitement and appreciation. I saw individuals there which I haven't seen for several years.

    This day that I am speaking of was my grandmother's 85th birthday celebration. My dad, along with others, put everything together in order to celebrate this wonderful day. This was going to be a surprise birthday celebration. Someone rented a hall to have the event. The theme of my grandmother's celebration was to "Give my grandmother flowers" while she was still alive. In most cases, a person will not receive those flowers from their loved ones until they are lying in a casket. At that time those flowers may not be as meaningful to the individual. This day was a lesson to me as I felt the power of love. Everyone came and gave flowers, cards, money and shared words of gratitude. Though this happened several years ago, it eventually gave me inspiration to write this book.

During the birthday celebration, a lot of family and friends came in support of my grandmother. Some came as far as Detroit and Philadelphia. We all waited at the hall patiently for my grandmother to arrive. We wanted to surprise her and yell "Happy Birthday" and maybe sing the birthday song. My grandmother is a very strong willed person. She can also be stubborn as well. Granny, if you are reading this please forgive me for saying that because you know that I love you! My grandmother is also a very loving person. After several attempts to get her to the hall, someone eventually told her that we were planning a surprise birthday celebration. When she arrived everyone was excited that she finally made it. My grandmother took the floor and shared her thoughts and appreciation for everything. She also informed us that it is not good to surprise the elderly because it may go wrong. She let everyone know that she doesn't like surprises. She went on to explain how a person may have a heart attack in that very moment. We all understood her words clearly. Immediately after she spoke, the celebration continued as planned.

My grandmother has been a strong influence in my life. She gave many words of wisdom during my childhood. I actually learned how to wake up every morning without an alarm clock from her. I can remember the many letters which she wrote me while I sat in prison serving time on a drug conviction. Her letters were no longer than a paragraph but they gave me strength to make it another day. She would start off with "I pray that this letter reaches you in the best of health and spirit." My grandmother continues to offer words of wisdom at her tender age of ninety-two. I am thankful and appreciative to have witnessed her life. Life is not promised to any of us from one day until the next. Actually, life is not promised to us from one second to the next. Granny, I reach these flowers to you as a small token in the form of a chapter in this book. These are your flowers!

Chapter 4

The Value of Family

There is value in family! We all have or have had family at one time in our lives. Our families were mostly given to us by God. I say mostly because there are exceptions to the rule. True value of family shines through during our most difficult times because they are the ones who offer assistance. The support of family is one of those "priceless" items which we share on earth. There may be times when we see this value and hold it close to our hearts. Then there's other times when we may question their existence. There are memories full of many different emotions associated with family. Sometimes family are the only ones that we can rely on. Then there are times when we question God for placing us in such a family dynamic.

Family may not always agree even on minor issues but they are a gift from the creator. I am thankful for my brothers, sisters, aunts, uncles, nieces and nephews. I am also thankful for the people whom I choose to call friends. Most importantly, I am thankful for my wife and children. Life has much more meaning when finding purpose. In finding purpose, I had to take a close look at myself and remind myself of what I wanted out of life. In finding my purpose, I was eventually led to my wife. It is a blessing for two souls to become one. According to the scriptures, a man must leave his mother and father and grab a hold unto his wife. I am very thankful for my wife and the many good things which I have to be thankful for.

I have to take this opportunity and thank God for my wife! She has been a blessing to me. I've learned many things from her. I know that she is the woman who God meant for me to be with. I was raised in the northeastern part of the country and my wife in the south. There are many things we can learn from one another. In marriage our goal is to continue to grow together. We are approaching another anniversary and I feel blessed to be with her. The small things are probably most important in a marriage. There are many good memories which I can discuss concerning our marriage! The most important memories are the times when we are enjoying the presence of one another and discussing life.

I am very thankful for my family and extended family. My wife and nine year old daughter add daily meaning to my life. I am also thankful for my oldest daughter and her children, though we are separated by more than 1,000 miles. On behalf of my wife, who is sole caretaker of her mother, we offer flowers to my mother-in-law as well. Our nine year old daughter appreciates the time that you share with her. You have a lot to offer the world.

I reach these flowers to my wife and the others as a small token of love in the form of this chapter. These are your flowers!

These Are Your Flowers

Chapter 5

Thank You!

I would like to start this chapter off by saying thank you to the many people who stood up for justice, in this country, in order for things to get better for us. These individuals stood up during a time when doing such a thing may cost their lives. Some of them paid the ultimate price. I say "thank you" to our popular leaders as well as the ones who may not have been as popular. I thank the many individual who paved the way such as: Fredrick Douglas, John Brown, Sojourner Truth, W.E.B. Dubois, Marcus Garvey, Booker T. Washington, Shirley Chisholm, Harriet Tubman, Rev. Dr. Martin Luther King Jr, Malcolm X, and many others. These individuals can be research in some of our history books found in public libraries. Those individuals dedicated their lives to fight for justice. I also thank those who stood up for justice in other countries such as Nelson Mandela and Mahatma Gandhi. Those who stand for justice anywhere ultimately stand for justice everywhere. We remember you, we honor you, and we thank you for doing such a great job for us. Those mentioned, along with others, made sacrifices in their lives in order to make our lives better. I may not have had the opportunity to freely write this or any other book, if it were not for you. Thank you!

I now thank those who are currently setting a positive example for others to follow. This consists of individuals that we may see and bypass each day. I also thank those who are working with our youth in order to prevent them from going down the wrong path. I thank those who are working with the elderly. It takes patience and love in order to care for others. I would also like to thank President Barack Obama for the courage which he had in order to overcome many obstacles and set a great example for others to follow. The game had been changed on this one. We can now truly say that "anything is possible!" I would also like to mention the brave men and women who have served and continue to serve in the United States Military. We thank you for making great sacrifices for this nation. Our prayers are that you will make it home safe to your families and that the United States Government will assist in your transition process.

I would like to acknowledge, Susannah Mushatt Jones, who is the oldest known *documented* person in the world, according to the Guinness book of records. She was born in 1899 on July 6th. Ms. Jones is now 116 years old. My youngest daughter shares the same birthday of July 6th with her. The second known *documented* living person, according to the Guinness book of records, is Emma Murano-Martinuzzi. She is currently 115 years old (Guinness 2015).

Once again I thank my wife, my grandmother, Ms. Tee, my mother, my step mother, my dad, my mother figures and many others. As I mentioned each of them in previous chapters, they have each been positive influences in my life. I would like to thank my dad's current wife, Ms.

Anny for all of her support and encouraging words. She has been a part of my life for many years and continues to offer guidance. I thank my younger brother's mother Ms. Cee for being one of those mother figures in my life. She continues to be just as nice to me now as she was when I meet her more than twenty-five years ago. I thank my cousin Jack Willie for our many interactions over the years. Cousin my words are not able to express all the things that I've learned from you. Each one of these individuals has contributed to my life in one way or another. I would like to take the time to thank everyone for everything that they've ever done for me.

Because of all that was done for me, I have become a better person. My life now has more meaning. I have started to position myself to receive the many blessings from God. I stood in my own way for many years while making poor decisions and blaming others for my failures. No, I am not perfect and I know that I still have a long way to go. I would like to live each day to the best of my ability without violating another human being.

I give flowers to all as a small token in the form of this chapter. I say thank you! These are your flowers!

Chapter 6

Here's Your Flowers

During the process of reflecting on giving flowers to my loved ones, I have a greater appreciation for life. I can now clearly see that life is delicate and may come to a sudden end. Life as we know it is a temporary gift for us while here on earth. We will have the opportunity to make the best of it until we are suddenly taken to a place which we only read about through scriptures. There is no particular known order in which this takes place. Anyone of us can be taken at any given time. Whether we are ready or not there is no coming back from it. Even then, life will continue to go on for everyone else.

I acknowledged several of my loved ones and gave out flowers! I said thank you to them as well. My dad and the others did a fantastic job in giving my grandmother her flowers during her 85th birthday celebration. I would like for this idea of love and support to continue on. I also encourage others to think about your own family and friends. The giving of flowers must not be limited to something which we do during a funeral. This would be a disservice to us and our loved ones.

There are times when we may become bogged down with everyday life. It seems that there is not enough time for family. We must take time out of our busy schedules in order to say to them "here's your flower!" I am hoping that this book will remind us to love, appreciate and give thanks to our loved ones.

Today, as a home, a community, a nation, and a society; we must find the time to give our loved ones their flowers while they are still alive. Remember that tomorrow is not promised to any of us. Whether young or old, our days are numbered. There is no day better than today to let our loved ones knows exactly how we feel about them. Think of your many loved ones and take the time to let them know just how much they mean to you. I know that I may not have said it as often as I should but there is no better day than today for me as well. I reach my hands out to you in love, saying I love you! I also say thank you! I may not be able to buy my wife a big house or a fancy car. I may not even be able to afford some of those fancy dresses, purses or watches but I know that you deserve those things. But I can make sure that you know that you are appreciated. With my hands reached out, I say to you that "these are your flowers."

To my readers and their families, these are your flowers! Share this with the ones that you love most. Make them feel special as you know they are deserving of it.

Reflect over your own loved ones and think about how you would feel if they were to suddenly pass on. Don't allow guilt to take hold of you in the end. Would you be able to honestly say that you said everything that you wanted or needed to say to them? Did you let them know exactly how you felt about them? Did you give them their flowers while they were living? I encourage you to take action now! We stretch our hands out to you in the form of this book, as a small token of appreciation for all that you've done for us! Let's say it together, "these are your flowers!"

It is not too late, as long as the person is still alive. Give them their flowers while they are here on earth. This book can be used as a reminder to give our loved ones their flower. `

These Are Your Flowers!

Outro

"These Are Your Flowers" is the first installment of the "Life Has Meaning Series." In writing this book, I hope to bring awareness of the importance of giving flowers to our loved ones. As far as I know, we only have one life to live. Hopefully, we can all make the best of our short time here. Showing appreciation to our loved ones may also bring a smile to their face.

This book is for all of my followers, friends and potential readers. This is for my dad, my mother, my step-mother, my grandmother, my wife, Ms. Tee, Ms. Cee, Ms. Anny and my cousin Jack Willie! This is also for the many individuals who have made a positive difference in my life. As I reach these flowers to you, I say "I love you!" I also say "Thank You!" Together with my audience of readers we say "We love you and appreciate all that you have done for us." We live in a society where everyone is so busy with their personal lives that we sometimes can't find the time for others.

I plan on releasing other books within this series in order to highlight some of the ways that adds meaning to life. Keep your eyes and ears open for the next installment of the "Life Has Meaning Series." Thank you for your support.

Books by the Author

These Are Your Flowers
    (Life Has Meaning Series: Book One)
100 Years: A Journey to End a Vicious Cycle

Books Are Available on Amazon!

About the Author

Mark L Baynard is a native of Wilmington, Delaware who currently lives in the State of Alabama. During his teenage years he got involved with the street life and made unwise decisions. His dealings extended to the streets of Philadelphia, North and South Jersey, and New York City. This eventually led him to prison. He took full responsibility for the mistakes which he made in his life and began making changes for the better. Once he was released, he later moved to Montgomery, Alabama with family in search of a fresh start. He met his wife whom they now share a nine year old daughter together. Mark has been working with troubled teenagers for the past nine years at different youth facilities. Mark furthered his education by earning an Associate Degree in Early Childhood Education and a Bachelor's Degree in Criminal Justice. He is currently pursuing his Master's

Degree in Public Administration. Mark started his writing career as a way to inform others of the dangers of falling into the cycle of crime and prison. His first effort is "100 Years: A Journey to End a Vicious Cycle." Mark's journey can be used as a testament to help others. "These Are Your Flowers" is the second book written by this author but it is the first book in the "Life Has Meaning Series." This is a series of short stories which will highlight meaningful things in life. Mark speaks about issues close to his heart within his writing. His words can be felt down to the soul! Mark's goal is to make a positive difference in our society. He also plans on continuing his career as an author. Stay tuned for other books as he refuse to stop now. The sky is the limit and he is reaching as high as he can.

Life Has Meaning Series

Life Has Meaning Series is the brain child of the Author, Mark L Baynard, and is full of great potential. Each book will consist of a short story which highlights something meaningful in life. We will now get to see another side of this amazing author. This series has the potential to captivate readers and take them on a ride from one book to the next. This series was established in an attempt to do a number of positive things in our society. One of which is to shed light on relevant issues which we may have the opportunity to address in our communities. My hope is that this series will encourage and motivate others to become better human beings. There is a need to bring more light into our world. Change sometimes happens in very small stages. None of us are perfect but we all have an opportunity to walk in a direction which may set a positive example. There are gifts within each of us, and I look forward to the fruit which will multiply."

References

(Guinness 2015)

http://www.guinnessworldrecords.com/

(Lean On Me, 1989) Lean On Me, the Movie

www.ingramcontent.com/pod-product-compliance
Lightning Source LLC
Chambersburg PA
CBHW060403050426
42449CB00009B/1871